CHRISTMAS ACROSTICS

21 Poems, Prayers, and
Questions for Reflection

SARAH CAYAS

Christmas Acrostics
21 Poems, Prayers, and Questions for Reflection

© Copyright 2024 by Sarah Cayas

Book cover created with Canva.

All rights reserved. No part of this publication may be reproduced in any form without written permission from the copyright owner.

ISBN: 978-1-0691999-1-1

For more information, email scpublishing.sc@gmail.com.

presented to

____

from

____

dated

____

Rainheart,
my love and partner in everything,
let us keep on shining the light of Jesus
and raising the next generation.

Sky,
my most beautiful Christmas gift ,
your life always declares God's glory.

Rain,
my handsome rainbow.
you can find God's grace and mercy
in the eye of the storm.

Snow,
my perfect witness that God quietly heals,
forever delight in His presence.
I will see you in heaven.

I love you all.

Table of Contents

The Grand Story

The Creator God
Has written a grand story
Every person has to know

Glory to God in the highest
Rejoice, praise His name
All who received Christ are
New creations
Destined to eternal life

Saviour and light of the nations
The baby who was born
On Earth, he lived, died and
Resurrected for Your salvation-
Your story is part of His Grand Story!

Suggested reading: **Psalm 67**

Prayer: God, be gracious to me and bless me, make Your face shine on me so that You and Your salvation will be known to all the nations.

Reflect: What song of joy can you sing to God so you can join the nations in praising Him?

Light of the World

"Let there be light!"
In the beginning, said God,
God spoke and all came to existence—
Heavens and Earth,
The whole universe, and all that is in it!

Oh, everything God made was good but
Fallen were humans of His glory.

Though the world became broken
He provided a solution— one and only,
Eternally grateful for Jesus Almighty!

Without Him, nothing was made that was made
Oh, He is the True Light,
        the Word who became flesh
Redeemer and Saviour, God's Holy lamb, the
Light that shines in the darkness, so
Darkness is forever overcome.

Suggested reading: **John 1**

Prayer: God Almighty, Spirit and Creator of the universe and everything in it, thank You for Jesus, the Word who became flesh, who gives light to this world in darkness. Jesus, the True Light, help me shine Your light.

Reflect: How can you shine the light of Jesus to those around you?

Bright Morning Star

Before it was darkness
Right before time began
In and through His Word
God created with
His Spirit and His Son
The universe is His and all is in His hands

Mighty God,
Overflowing with love, despite of sin
Redeemed the world through Jesus
Now in Him, we are alive
In His grace, we are saved
Now and forevermore
Glory to God, to Him we belong

Soon, He is coming
The bright Morning star
Alpha and Omega
Riding from the clouds

Suggested reading: **Revelation 22:12-16**

Prayer: Oh Alpha and Omega, the Root and Offspring of David, the bright Morning Star, thank You for washing my sins with your blood. Thank You, my Redeemer and Friend.

Reflect: Who can you introduce to Jesus, so they can experience His love and light?

A Child is Born

All the world celebrates

Christ Jesus, the Saviour's birth
He who was born naked
Incarnated, with us He dwelt
Lived as a man, though fully God
Died for the glory of His Dad

In Him by faith, we are saved
Since He had conquered death

Beloved, soon He will come again
On the clouds riding from heaven
Reigning our hearts majestically
Now and forever He will be.

Suggested reading: **Isaiah 9:6-7**

Prayer: Wonderful Counselor, Mighty God, Everlasting Father, Prince of Peace, You are just and righteous and Your kingdom will never end. Reign in me.

Reflect: In what way can you reflect God's justice and righteousness in your life?

Jesus Christ

Jesus Christ
Eternal God the Son
Supreme and Lord
Unchanging
Saviour of the world

Celebrate
His humble birth
Rejoice
In His appearing
Sing all the earth
To the King of all kings

Suggested reading: **Matthew 1:18-24**

Prayer: Shepherd of my soul, my Lord, and King, I worship You, my God. Help me seek You with all my heart, You are my joy and strength.

Reflect: What treasures can you offer to Jesus?

Jesus was Born

Jesus was born
Emmanuel, God with us
Saviour of the world,
Ultimate sacrifice
So from death to life, we pass

Whoever believes in Christ
All who call on His name
Salvation and eternal life are His amazing grace

Because He lived, died, and rose again
Over death and evil, He's victorious
Returning to the world to reign
Now and forever, He's glorious!

Suggested reading: **Luke 2**

Prayer: Sovereign Lord, oh Father, let me be like Jesus in Your house, sitting among the teachers, listening and asking questions. Help me grow and become strong, be filled with wisdom, full of Your grace, in favour with You and others.

Reflect: In what area of your life can you grow to be like Jesus?

Love Gives Love

Listen, all nations:
Open your heart to Jesus!
Victory, forgiveness, joy, love,
Eternal Life is found in Him.

Go and proclaim it!
In Christ alone
Verily through faith
Each of us is
Saved by His grace.

Love gives love;
Oh yes, God did when He gave Jesus,
Very true is His promise,
Even death won't separate us from His love.

Suggested reading: **Ephesians 2:4-10**

Prayer: Thank you for Your great love, oh God of love. You are rich in mercy and kindness and I will be forever grateful for the gift of Christ and being made alive in Him.

Reflect: How does experiencing God's great love and mercy change your perspective in life?

Crazy Love

Christ Jesus is coming soon-
Rejoice, I will say it again rejoice!
All the earth bows down and worship
Zion, rejoice, let all the nations be glad!
Yes, sing praise to the Lord Almighty!

Lord of lords, King of kings
Oh come, Emmanuel; for the
Veil of the temple was torn by Your
Extravagant crazy love.

Suggested reading: **Mark 15:37-39**

Prayer: Son of God, my Lord and Saviour, thank You for dying on the cross for my sins. You are the Lamb of God who laid down Your life freely so I can escape eternal death. Jesus, You tore the veil.

Reflect: What difference does it make that you can approach God's throne of grace with confidence?

Christmas Giving

Christmas is about giving
Have you heard?
Rejoice for Jesus was born, yes
It brings joy to the heart!
Son of God was given
To the world-
May it not be forgotten,
A loving, generous Father gave
So we will be saved.

Give thanks!
Indeed, God is gracious
Victory is in Christ
In Him, we live forever,
Nothing can separate us from
God's great love.

Suggested reading: **Romans 8:28-39**

Prayer: Search my heart, oh loving God. Father, You graciously gave Your Son for me so I can be forgiven. Spirit and Jesus, thank You for interceding for me and that nothing can separate me from Your love.

Reflect: In what weakness do you need God's help?

Jesus Christ Loves You

Jesus, I adore You
Everlasting God
Sun and shield
Universe Maker
Shine Your light

Crown of Glory
Hosanna in the Highest
Righteous One
Immanuel
Saviour of the world
Take my heart

Lover of my soul
Overflow
Very Present Help
Exceeding Great Reward
Secure me in Your arms

You are my all
Overflowing and
Unending is Your love

Suggested reading: **Psalm 45**

Prayer: Jesus Christ, my bridegroom. Thank You for laying down Your life for me. You captivate my heart, I am Yours.

Reflect: How do you magnify God's beauty as a bride of Christ?

Jesus Heals

Just as we celebrate Jesus' birth
Earth is rejoicing but not quite yet
Silent night most people wish,
Unity, love, and peace.
Soon, the Prince of Peace will return,

He who heals us through all our pain.
Everyone is invited to His kingdom
All nations will gather at His throne,
Let's patiently wait on God alone
Shine His light and make Him known!

Suggested reading: **Isaiah 53**

Prayer: Thank You, Lord Jesus, for taking my pain and bearing my suffering. I was lost but now I am found. In You, I have peace.

Reflect: What pain do you have, which you can bring at the foot of the cross?

When Home is Far Away

When home is far away on Christmas
Heartbeats mixed with gladness and
homesickness while
Earth reminisces the
Nativity of Christ Jesus-

Heaven, He left to
Obey the Father
Manger was His cradle
Equality with God He did not consider

In being found in appearance as a man
Servant is what He had become

For Christ was born to save the world
And lived to die once and for all to
Redeem and reconcile us to the Lord

And though my home is far as it may seem
With Christ I'm home, I'll rejoice and sing
And celebrate my God and King and
Yearn for His second coming!

Suggested reading: **Philippians 2:5-11**

Prayer: Jesus, You left Your home in heaven so I can be home with You. My heart yearns for you. Thank You for being with me always.

Reflect: How can you serve your home and influence the next generation by following Jesus' example?

I am a Stranger in This Land and He as Well

I am a stranger in this land

And He as well when He became like us,
Messiah, the Anointed One,

Alpha and Omega became man.

Sights of sparkling snow
Tall pine trees and other evergreens
Raindrops turn to flurries
As I walk through the chilly wind,
Newcomers from various nations
Gather together and celebrate
Each of these is a lovely surprise
Reckoning the joy in my heart

I may be longing for something else
Nobody can give but

The only reason for this season is
He alone indeed
I know that's why He came,
Stranger, He was, but not anymore; His

Life He freely offered
And that's what friends are for.
Now, His gift of friendship and His
Dear life is for you too

Accept it please or have you? His promise is
Never will He abandon you.
Diadem of beauty,

Heaven's most precious one,
Everlasting King

And the Father's begotten Son,
Star of the morning shining bright

With His eternal light,
Everything else is found in Him-
Love and friendship that
Lasts forever and for life.

Suggested reading: **John 15:9-17**

Prayer: You are my greatest friend and Saviour, Jesus. Thank You for Your great love. Help me remain in Your love by living the Father's will.

Reflect: How can you extend the love of Jesus to a stranger?

Christmas in Our Hearts

Come, let us adore Him
He who is God yet became man
Rock of our salvation
Immanuel, God the Son
Sing, praise, and worship
The Lord of lords and King of kings
Maker of the universe
And all of the amazing things
Seek first His kingdom

In our hearts, we can find
Not of this world but through His Spirit

Our will to His aligns; He is the
Uncovered mystery of old
Recalled, reminisced, and retold

Hosanna in the Highest
Ever Holy is the LORD
As we celebrate this Christmas
Remember those who are hurting
The reason why Jesus came-
So, all can experience His healing.

Suggested reading: **Luke 5:27-32**

Prayer: Jesus, You are the friend of sinners. You came to heal the broken. Thank You, for calling me to follow You.

Reflect: In what way can you bring God's comfort to those who are suffering?

Waiting for Jesus

Wishing you love, joy,
And peace
In this festive
Time of the year;
I pray for you
Never-ending
Grace,

Faith, and
Of all heavenly dear...
Ready yourselves as

Jesus is coming again,
Eagerly wait for Him as you
Share His good news to humankind
Until all nations will hear, be
Still and know that He is God and near.

Suggested reading: **Psalm 46**

Prayer: Help me, God, to be still and know who You are. Thank You for being my refuge and strength. I exalt You.

Reflect: How can you practice stillness in times of trouble?

Jesus is Our Hope

Jesus is our hope
Everyone comes to seek Him-
Saviour and our Lord, the
Ultimate gift of God-
Sing to the King of Kings!

If your heart is anxious in this troubled time
Sit in His quiet presence,
       long for His kingdom to come

Our hope is in Jesus
Unending is His love
Remember He's coming again
      from the heavens above

Hail to the Lord of lords, Alpha and
Omega, the First and the Last
Prince of Peace, Ancient of Days
Emmanuel, God is with us!

Suggested reading: **John 14:26-27**

Prayer: Oh, Jesus, Prince of Peace, thank You for giving me Your peace. Spirit of God, thank You for teaching me all things.

Reflect: What are you learning right now that helps you overcome your fear?

Come, Lord Jesus

Christmas is here
Once again,
Merry Christmas never
Ends.

Lord Jesus came.
One day, He will
Return;
Diadem of Beauty, forever He'll reign.

Joy to the world
Every nation is called
So, let us make Him known, let
Us proclaim Lord Jesus, come,
So, come.

Suggested reading: **Revelation 22:17-21**

Prayer: I wait for You, Jesus, my bridegroom. You are my Life. Help me remember that You are coming soon.

Reflect: How are you preparing for the Lord's return?

Home This Christmas

Here we come to our
Old familiar haven where
Memories are refreshed through
Every sight and taste.

The loved ones we missed,
Home buddies and friends, we
Instantly connect, the moment we
See them.

Christmas
Here and everywhere is
Remembering Christ's
Incarnation, and then his
Second coming too,
To all who long for His return.
Merry Christmas
And happy cheers,
Sweet blessings to you.

Suggested reading: **John 14:23-24**

Prayer: Father, thank You for loving me and making Your home with me. Help me to obey Jesus' teachings always.

Reflect: How do you bring Jesus to your earthly home to make it heavenly?

Merry Christmas

Merry Christmas
Everyone
Rejoice in the Lord
Rejoice, I will say it again
Yes, you who are saved!

Christ Jesus came and
He will be returning
Redeemer and Lord
I pray over you His blessing
Shine His light
To all peoples
Make known His name
And wait for His second coming
So hope, while you proclaim

Suggested reading: **Philippians 4:4-7**

Prayer: Oh Lord, You are near. I rejoice and thank You that You have written my name in Your book of life. May Your peace guard my heart and mind in Christ Jesus.

Reflect: What requests do you need to present to God to overcome your anxiety and experience His peace?

Joyful Christmas

Joyful Christmas, all
Over the world
Yearn for Christ's return
For every nation is called,
Unfailing is His promise
Loving to young and old.

Come, let us adore Him
He is coming back
Redeemer and our Saviour
Immanuel, He's the Rock,
See, He will reign forever
To Him, all glory belongs
Most High King
And Lord of lords
Sing Him worshipful songs.

Suggested reading: **John 16:20-24**

Prayer: Jesus, I long for that day when I do not need to ask for anything when no one can take away my joy. For You are my joy and my joy is complete in You.

Reflect: Where in your life do you need to experience the joy of Jesus?

It has been a Year

It has been a year
Time flew indeed so fast

Holidays are here
Again, but then they won't last
So, I pray for a blessed Christmas and

Bounty blessings for you
Everyday provisions for
Each of your loved ones, too;
Not only for the season but

All year round I hope

You'll always be
Excited, waiting for Jesus Christ our Lord
As you share His grace and
Redeeming love, such is awesome to behold!

Suggested reading: **Isaiah 43**

Prayer: Lord God, You are my Creator and Redeemer. I am glad that I am Yours. Thank you that I do not have to dwell in the past for You are doing a new thing.

Reflect: How is God making a way for you as He unfolds His will for your life?

About the Author

Sarah Cayas is a life and career coach and an online mentor. She has over 20 years of experience in Christian ministries including Power to Change and Discipleship International. She has mainly served in Canada and the Philippines and engaged short-term in parts of Asia, Africa, and North and South America. She holds a Bachelor of Arts degree with disciplines in theatre arts and creative writing. She is also a minister with the Christian Leaders Alliance. Sarah resides with her family in Winnipeg, Manitoba, Canada.

Kindly Review!

Thank you for reading my anthology!
I appreciate all of your feedback and I love hearing what you have to say. I need your input to make the next version of this book (and my future books) better.
Please take a minute now to leave a helpful review on Amazon or my Facebook page and let me know what you think of the book:

amazon.com/author/sarah.cayas
facebook.com/sarah.cayas.fb

Thank you so much,
Sarah

www.ingramcontent.com/pod-product-compliance
Lightning Source LLC
Chambersburg PA
CBHW061315140726
47998CB00006B/2397